I0804443

The INSIDE GUIDE

STEM IN SPORTS

STEM in Ice Hockey

By Beatrice Harris

Cavendish Square

Published in 2025 by Cavendish Square Publishing, LLC
2544 Clinton Street Buffalo, NY 14224

Copyright © 2025 by Cavendish Square Publishing, LLC

No part of this publication may be reproduced, stored in a retrieval system, or transmitted in any form or by any means—electronic, mechanical, photocopying, recording, or otherwise—without the prior permission of the copyright owner. Request for permission should be addressed to Permissions, Cavendish Square Publishing, 2544 Clinton Street Buffalo, NY 14224. Tel (877) 980-4450; fax (877) 980-4454.

Website: cavendishsq.com

This publication represents the opinions and views of the author based on their personal experience, knowledge, and research. The information in this book serves as a general guide only. The author and publisher have used their best efforts in preparing this book and disclaim liability rising directly or indirectly from the use and application of this book.

Disclaimer: Portions of this work were originally authored by Ryan Nagelhout and published as *The Science of Hockey* (Sports Science). All new material this edition authored by Beatrice Harris.

All websites were available and accurate when this book was sent to press.

Library of Congress Cataloging-in-Publication Data

Names: Harris, Beatrice, author.
Title: STEM in ice hockey / Beatrice Harris.
Description: Buffalo, New York : Cavendish Square Publishing, [2025] |
Series: The inside guide: STEM in sports | Includes index.
Identifiers: LCCN 2023052204 (print) | LCCN 2023052205 (ebook) | ISBN 9781502671288 (library binding) | ISBN 9781502671271 (paperback) | ISBN 9781502671295 (ebook)
Subjects: LCSH: Hockey–Juvenile literature. | Science–Study and teaching–Juvenile literature. | Sports science–Juvenile literature.
Classification: LCC GV847.25 .H36 2025 (print) | LCC GV847.25 (ebook) | DDC 796.962–dc23/eng/20231204
LC record available at https://lccn.loc.gov/2023052204
LC ebook record available at https://lccn.loc.gov/2023052205

Editor: Therese Shea
Copyeditor: Danielle Haynes
Designer: Deanna Lepovich

The photographs in this book are used by permission and through the courtesy of: Cover Steve Gilbert/Shutterstock.com; p. 4 Gorodenkoff/Shutterstock.com; pp. 6 (main), 16, 19 Jai Agnish/Shutterstock.com; p. 6 (inset) Sergey Zaykov/Shutterstock.com; p. 7 photographer2222/Shutterstock.com; p. 8 (left) Sergey Spritnyuk/Shutterstock.com; p. 8 (right) SebStock/Shutterstock.com; pp. 10, 12, 29 (top) Eugene Onischenko/Shutterstock.com; p. 13 Robert Nyholm/Shutterstock.com; p. 14 Grushin/Shutterstock.com; p. 15 Pressmaster/Shutterstock.com; p. 18 MACH Photos/Shutterstock.com; p. 20 Pavel L Photo and Video/Shutterstock.com; p. 21 Dmitry Niko/Shutterstock.com; p. 22 Nicholas Piccillo/Shutterstock.com; p. 24 Agris Krusts/Shutterstock.com; p. 25 VectorMine/Shutterstock.com; p. 27 Alexander Kochkin/Shutterstock.com; p. 28 (top) kovop/Shutterstock.com; p. 28 (bottom) Sergey Kuznecov/Shutterstock.com; p. 29 (bottom) SeventyFour/Shutterstock.com.

Some of the images in this book illustrate individuals who are models. The depictions do not imply actual situations or events.

CPSIA compliance information: Batch #CSCSQ25: For further information contact Cavendish Square Publishing LLC at 1-877-980-4450.

Printed in the United States of America

Find us on

CONTENTS

A hockey puck can travel as fast as 100 miles (160 kilometers) per hour!

Chapter One

A STEM SPORT

The high-speed sport of ice hockey is popular in many parts of the world. Spectators know they'll see hard hits, astonishing saves, and amazing shots in every game. But do they know they're watching STEM (science, **technology**, engineering, and math) in action? Now you do!

You need to be fast, strong, and tough to play hockey. You also need to be smart. Knowing the STEM ideas behind the sport can help you better understand the action on the ice.

Skate Science

Ice hockey is different from other sports because it features players with sharp blades on their feet zipping around on a sheet of ice. Hockey players often skate from one end of the **rink** to the other to score a goal or stop the other team from scoring. STEM ideas can teach us about the movements of the players on the ice.

For example, physics is a science that helps explain how players move the way they do. Physics is

Fast Fact

In North America, many of the best hockey players can be found in the National Hockey League (NHL).

Pro players from around the world play in the NHL, which has teams in both the United States and Canada.

There are different kinds of ice skates. Hockey skates are like boots with blades attached to the bottom.

the science of energy and matter and how they interact. Some physics terms aid us in describing matter in motion, including hockey players and pucks.

Speed, Velocity, Momentum

Speed is the rate at which an object travels a distance. Velocity is the rate at which an object changes its overall position. What's the difference? When we say that pro hockey players can skate as fast as 20 miles (32 km) per hour, we're talking about their speed. To talk about their velocity, we need to figure out their displacement, or how much they've changed

Hockey players turn their feet and cut into the ice to slow down or stop quickly.

THE FORCE OF FRICTION

What can slow down a hockey player? Forces can! A force is a push or pull on an object. Friction is a force of resistance. It tries to stop one object from sliding or rolling over another. Friction exists between a hockey player's skate blades and the ice. Hockey players have the blades sharpened to reduce friction. The less friction between the blade and the ice, the faster the player will be able to skate. After many people skate on the ice, the surface exerts, or puts forth, more friction. Luckily, an ice resurfacing machine can smooth it out again. You'll read more about this technology in Chapter 3.

A player can skate much faster on the rink on the left than the one on the right.

Fast Fact

Players put tape on the blade of their stick to create friction that helps them control the puck. They also put tape on the shaft of their stick so the stick doesn't slip from their hands.

position. This might still be 20 miles per hour if the player has only moved in one direction, but if they moved forward and backward, for example, it will be a different measurement. Velocity also includes a direction, such as east or north.

Now let's talk momentum. Momentum is mass in motion. All objects have mass, the term used for the amount of matter in something. It's often measured in units such as pounds or kilograms. An object—or a hockey player—has momentum when in motion. Math can help us figure out how much momentum when we multiply mass by velocity. Hockey players in motion often have more momentum than other athletes because they move at such high velocities.

Fast Fact

Acceleration is another physics term used in sports—often incorrectly! A hockey player is accelerating when their velocity is changing as they move down the ice.

Hockey players need sticks that are both strong and light.

Chapter Two

STICKS AND PUCKS

A hockey player's stick is as important to them as their skates. After all, the stick is the piece of technology they use to move the puck around and score (or keep their opponent from scoring). That might sound funny if you think of technology only as something electronic. However, technology is anything created using scientific knowledge that is meant to serve a purpose. Today's hockey sticks fit that explanation.

While early hockey sticks were made of wood, modern players use composite sticks, which are sticks made from different materials, such as a form of carbon called graphite. Graphite strands are pressed together to make the stick strong but still able to flex, or bend. Some sticks are engineered with two pieces, with a blade and shaft that are glued together. Others were crafted as one piece.

Fast Fact

Ready for more math? A hockey stick's shaft usually should not be longer than 63 inches (160 centimeters), according to the official NHL rule book. Taller players can ask for a stick 2 inches (5 cm) longer.

Slap Shot Science

A hockey stick's flexibility, or flex, is the key to taking big shots. Flex measures how much a stick will bend when a force is applied to it.

CURVED FOR CONTROL

Hockey sticks curve to the left or right for left-handed and right-handed players. The NHL states that stick blades can't curve more than 0.75 inch (19 millimeters) from a blade's heel to its toe. Why curve a stick's blade in the first place? Curved blades give a player more control over the puck. It's easier to lift a puck off the ice with a curved stick. A curved stick also gives a puck more spin when it's shot. This makes the puck more stable while it's moving so it lands flat. A spinning puck also experiences less air resistance, a kind of friction.

The sticks goaltenders, or goalies, use to stop pucks are different from the sticks used by other players. They're wide and flat on the bottom. This shape helps them block the net when the other team is trying to score.

Fast Fact

An applied force is a push or pull one object exerts on another. Shooting the puck with a stick is an example of applied force.

You can see how the hockey stick bends in this photo.

The slap shot is the fastest and hardest shot in hockey. Players wind up and shoot the puck as hard as they can, using a motion similar to a golf swing. When taking a slap shot, a hockey player should hit the ice with their stick before they hit the puck. This makes the stick bend, or flex, and allows energy to build up in the stick. When the stick unbends, this stored energy pushes the puck with a great amount of force.

Fast Fact

A tiny crack or chip in a hockey stick can cause it to break when it's flexed or hit by another player's stick. Even a small mistake when making a stick can cause it to snap without warning.

Energy on the Ice

The slap shot (and any shot) can help us understand the two main kinds of energy: potential and kinetic. Potential energy is stored energy. Kinetic energy is moving energy.

A moving hockey stick has kinetic energy. This kinetic energy turns to potential energy when the stick blade briefly stops on the ice. Then, it moves again, transferring its kinetic energy to the puck, exerting the force that makes the puck move. The still puck's potential energy then transforms into kinetic energy.

According to a law of physics called Newton's first law of

Hockey pucks have a shape that allows them to move easily across the ice.

motion, the puck will continue to move in a line at a constant speed until an outside force acts on it. Another player, such as a goalie, may stop it. If it's in the air, it will come down because of the force of gravity. If it's sliding on the ice, it will slow down because of friction between the puck and the ice. A hockey puck also may be stopped by the net in the goal, which means someone scored!

The movements of a hockey puck can be explained by Isaac Newton's laws of motion, which he published in 1687.

NHL players skate as much as 5 miles (8 km) per game!

ON THE ICE

Chapter Three

The ice is a **critical** part of an ice hockey game. Without the ice, the game wouldn't have the speed and the excitement that it does. The ice must be just right in order for hockey players to perform at the highest levels. Making that perfect ice takes knowledge of water as both a solid and a liquid matter.

Recipe for an Ice Rink

A hockey rink's engineers make ice that's strong enough to withstand 20 minutes of hard skating before it can be resurfaced. An ice surface starts with a big slab of concrete. Within this concrete, a saltwater **solution** is pumped through a system of pipes. This salty water freezes at a lower temperature than regular water does, so it doesn't freeze in the pipes but is cold enough to freeze the water on top of the concrete floor.

At the beginning of each season, workers spray a thin layer of water onto the concrete a little at a time. They **filter** the water many times to remove excess oxygen and minerals before spraying it to make ice. The water

Fast Fact

Ice hockey is just one kind of hockey. Some people play hockey on different surfaces, including grass and concrete.

Ice rinks that freeze naturally outdoors are said to use natural ice. Those frozen with technology are said to use artificial ice.

needs to freeze quickly to keep from getting dirty. **Impurities** make the ice weaker. Too much oxygen or too many minerals in the water can cause skate blades to sink into the ice because it's too soft. Ice makers want clean, clear ice that stays strong over long periods of use.

The first layer of ice is called a bond. The second layer is frozen to it and then painted white. The third layer is frozen over that. Lines, pictures, and writing are painted on the fourth layer. Eight or more layers are added on top of this layer. Each layer is so thin that all together, the ice is only about 1 inch (2.5 cm) thick! This whole process can take about 48 hours.

A standard NHL ice rink is an oval that's 200 feet (61 meters) long and 85 feet (26 m) wide. All lines and circles are carefully marked using certain measurements too.

Fast Fact

Too much oxygen in water is what causes ice cubes to be cloudy instead of clear.

Slick Surface

As players skate up and down the ice, carving into it, the ice becomes harder to skate on quickly and smoothly. Skates create holes and cuts in the ice too.

After each 20-minute period of a game, one or two ice resurfacing machines come out on the ice. They shave off the top layer and

THE WEATHER INSIDE

An ice surface's biggest enemy is the heat and **humidity** in an arena. When an empty arena fills with people, the climate inside changes and affects the ice. Most NHL arenas try to stay between 50 and 60 degrees Fahrenheit (10 and 16 degrees Celsius). Arenas have systems to balance humidity. If there's too little humidity, the ice can become **brittle**. Too much humidity allows moisture with impurities to sit on the ice. Modern NHL arenas are climate controlled, and workers constantly monitor arena conditions. Huge machines are used to pump outside air into the rink as needed.

The ice temperature in a hockey arena is around 24°F (-4°C).

People often call the ice resurfacing machine a Zamboni, but Zamboni is actually the company that makes these kinds of machines.

collect the shavings in a tank. They clean the ice with water and then collect dirt and water. Finally, they shoot hot water out the back. This water melts the top layer of ice a bit, and then it freezes into a new, smooth sheet.

Fast Fact

During the 1975 Stanley Cup Finals, the arena in Buffalo, New York, became too hot. Fog formed over the ice—even the players had a hard time seeing the puck!

Because ice hockey is such a fast sport, staying safe on the ice is essential. Players wear a lot of pads under their jerseys to protect themselves from injuries.

STAYING SAFE

Chapter Four

Over the years, hockey equipment has improved, helping players avoid more injuries. Still, the forces at work on the ice can be dangerous and even deadly.

Essential Equipment

Safety equipment such as shoulder pads, elbow pads, and helmets are just as important as skates and sticks to a hockey player. Shoulder pads are more than just shoulder protection. They include a collarbone protector; bicep (upper arm) protector; a chest, spine, and back protector; rib guards; and an abdominal (stomach) pad.

Fast Fact

A concussion is a serious brain injury that can happen due to **collisions** in hockey, such as two players crashing or a player's head hitting the boards around the rink. Helmets help but can't yet prevent concussions.

Pads are made of foam, plastic, and fabric pieces. The foam provides cushioning, and the plastic helps distribute some of the impact force of a collision. If the force is distributed, or spread out, it's less likely to cause injury.

In hockey, a body check is when a defensive player crashes into the opponent with the puck on purpose. They lead with their hip or shoulder.

Collision Course

When two hockey players skate toward one another at high speeds, collisions can occur. An elastic collision occurs when no kinetic energy is lost after two objects come together. Inelastic collisions occur when kinetic energy changes into a different kind of energy, such as sound or heat energy. For example, when two hockey players collide, some of their kinetic energy is changed to sound energy. That's how we're able to hear big hits at a hockey game.

No large collisions are perfectly elastic in our world. Small amounts of kinetic energy change into other forms of energy whenever two objects collide.

Kinds of Collisions

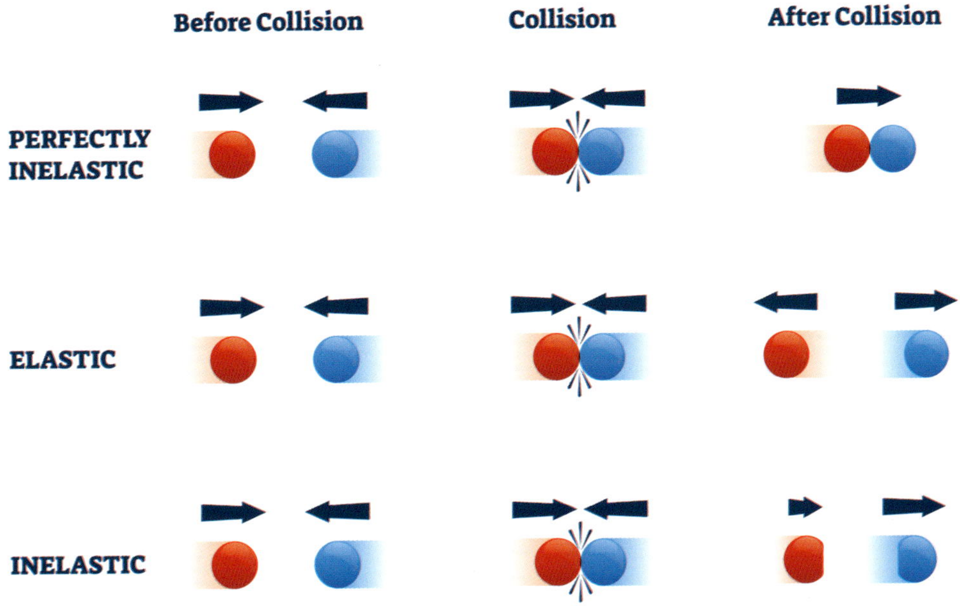

In inelastic collisions, momentum is conserved, or remains constant, but kinetic energy is lost. In a perfectly inelastic collision, the objects continue their momentum as one. In elastic collisions, momentum and kinetic energy are conserved.

Fast Fact

According to Newton's third law of motion, for every action, there is an equal and opposite reaction. That includes actions such as checking.

Goalie Gear

Goaltenders wear the most equipment because pucks are shot right at them. Even with all that padding, stopping a slap shot can hurt! Goaltenders wear much bigger chest protectors than other hockey players. They wear special gloves on each hand too.

SKATE BLADES

Ice skate blades are made of steel. The bottom of the blade isn't flat—it's concave, which means it curves inward. Usually, a team's equipment manager sharpens players' blades using a machine with a rotating stone wheel. As the wheel turns, it carves out the middle of the skate's blade bottom until there are two sharp edges. This process is called hollow grinding. To further reduce friction, the final step of skate sharpening is to oil the blade. Players decide how often they want their skates sharpened and how much of a hollow grind they want. A deeper hollow means more grip but slower movement.

The hand they hold their stick with also uses a blocker, which has a hard, flat surface to stop the puck's motion. A goaltender wears a glove similar to a baseball glove on their other hand. They use the glove to catch the puck.

Goalie pads need to be light and flexible to allow the player a wide range of motion while keeping them safe. Water-resistant leather or plastic keeps the pads from getting wet and heavier because of the ice.

STEM on Ice

Science, technology, engineering, and math are always at work when hockey players take the ice. Even the crystal-clear ice they skate on takes STEM knowledge and skills to create.

Fast Fact

A goaltender's job is to stop the puck as it follows its trajectory to the net. A trajectory is the path an object takes in the air.

Many goalie masks are made with fiberglass and Kevlar, which is the same material used in bulletproof vests.

The more you watch hockey and study STEM, the more you'll see it's a STEM game. The ideas behind skating, passing, and shooting all work together to create the big hits, superior saves, lightning-fast skating, and wild goals that make a hockey game so exciting.

THINK ABOUT IT!

1. Name a technology at a hockey game that wasn't mentioned in this book. How would the game be different without it?

2. Do you think friction can be helpful in a hockey game? Explain.

3. Explain how knowledge of math is important in a hockey game.

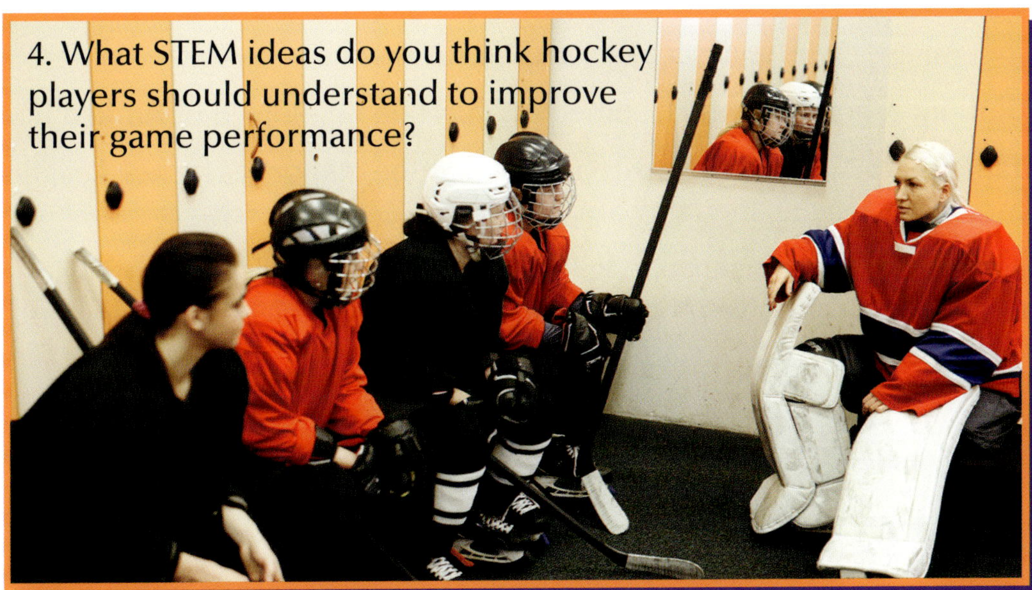

4. What STEM ideas do you think hockey players should understand to improve their game performance?

GLOSSARY

brittle: Easily broken when stressed.

collision: The action of two or more things or people crashing into each other.

critical: Very important.

essential: Necessary and important.

fiberglass: A strong, light material made from thin glass threads.

filter: To collect bits from a liquid passing through.

humidity: Moisture in the air.

impurity: Unwanted matter found in something, which prevents it from being pure.

reaction: The force that an object subjected to an outside force exerts in the opposite direction.

rink: An area with a surface of ice used for skating.

solution: A liquid in which something has been dissolved or broken up.

Stanley Cup: The trophy that is awarded to the National Hockey League team that wins the annual championship.

technology: Using science, engineering, and other industries to invent useful tools or to solve problems. Also, a machine, piece of equipment, or method created by technology.

FIND OUT MORE

Books

Ellenport, Craig. *Hockey: Score with STEM!* Minneapolis, MN: Bearport Publishing Company, 2022.

Gitlin, Marty. *The Hockey Book of Why (and Who, What, When, Where, and How): The Answers to Questions You've Always Wondered About the Fastest Game on Ice*. Essex, CT: Lyons Press, 2023.

Stark, Kristy. *STEM in the Stanley Cup*. Minneapolis, MN: Abdo Publishing, 2020.

Websites

Rookie Road: Ice Hockey Basic Rules for Kids
www.rookieroad.com/ice-hockey/basic-rules-for-kids
Find out how to play hockey as well as how to understand the action on the ice better.

Sports Engine: The Science of NHL Hockey: Slapshots
www.sportsengine.com/ice-hockey/science-nhl-hockey-slapshots
Read more about the STEM behind this exciting shot.

Wonderopolis: What Are Hockey Pucks Made Of?
wonderopolis.org/wonder/what-are-hockey-pucks-made-of
Check out interesting facts about hockey pucks, such as where they're made.

Publisher's note to educators and parents: Our editors have carefully reviewed these websites to ensure that they are suitable for students. Many websites change frequently, however, and we cannot guarantee that a site's future contents will continue to meet our high standards of quality and educational value. Be advised that students should be closely supervised whenever they access the internet.

INDEX